Ellen Ochoa

Dynamic Space Director

Rebecca Felix

Checkerboard Library

An Imprint of Abdo Publishing
abdobooks.com

ABDOBOOKS.COM

Published by Abdo Publishing, a division of ABDO, PO Box 398166, Minneapolis, Minnesota 55439.
Copyright © 2019 by Abdo Consulting Group, Inc. International copyrights reserved in all countries.
No part of this book may be reproduced in any form without written permission from the publisher.
Checkerboard Library™ is a trademark and logo of Abdo Publishing.

Printed in the United States of America, North Mankato, Minnesota
102018
012019

THIS BOOK CONTAINS RECYCLED MATERIALS

Design: Kelly Doudna, Mighty Media, Inc.
Production: Mighty Media, Inc.
Editor: Liz Salzmann
Front Cover Photographs: NASA (both)
Back Cover Photographs: NASA (Aldrin, ISS, space shuttle, Apollo rocket), Shutterstock (planets)
Interior Photographs: AP Images, pp. 19 (top left), 27; Grossmont High School Museum, pp. 9, 11, 28 (bottom left);
NASA, pp. 5, 7, 13, 17, 19 (top right, bottom left, bottom center), 21, 23, 25, 28 (bottom right), 29 (top, bottom);
Sandia Lab News, pp. 15, 28 (top); Tksteven/Wikimedia Commons, p. 19 (bottom right)

Library of Congress Control Number: 2018948904

Publisher's Cataloging-in-Publication Data
Names: Felix, Rebecca, author.
Title: Ellen Ochoa: dynamic space director / by Rebecca Felix.
Other title: Dynamic space director
Description: Minneapolis, Minnesota : Abdo Publishing, 2019 | Series: Space
    crusaders | Includes online resources and index.
Identifiers: ISBN 9781532117039 (lib. bdg.) | ISBN 9781532159879 (ebook)
Subjects: LCSH: Ochoa, Ellen--Juvenile literature. | Astronauts--United States--
    Biography--Juvenile literature. | Space Shuttle Discovery--Juvenile literature. |
    Lyndon B. Johnson Space Center--Juvenile literature.
Classification: DDC 629.450 [B]--dc23

Contents

1 Space Maestro

Ellen Ochoa is a space and science pioneer. She is an accomplished astronaut. And she leads thousands of other astronauts and scientists at **NASA**.

Since 1993, Ochoa has traveled into space four times and spent almost 1,000 hours there. Her first trip made history. Ochoa was the first woman of Hispanic descent to go into space. During her space missions, Ochoa put her science and computer skills to work.

Back on Earth, Ochoa continued to make history. In 2012, she became the first Hispanic director of NASA's Lyndon B. Johnson Space Center (JSC). She is only the second woman to hold this title.

Space travel and leadership were not Ochoa's first successes. Before NASA, she helped create three patented scientific inventions. She was also a classical flute player. Ochoa credits her achievements to her education, which she took seriously from a young age.

② Star Student

Ellen Ochoa was born on May 10, 1958 in Los Angeles, California. She spent most of her early life in La Mesa, California. Ellen considers this city her hometown. She has four **siblings**. Ellen's mother, Rosanne Ochoa, raised them on her own. Ellen's father left the family when Ellen was young. It is from him the Ochoa children received their Mexican **heritage**.

Raising five children kept Rosanne busy. But continuing her education was important to her. Rosanne took one college class at a time throughout Ellen's childhood. She studied everything from biology to business. Rosanne's devotion to learning made a strong impression on Ellen and her siblings. The Ochoa children did well in school. Ellen was especially good at writing, math, and science.

In 1969, when Ellen was 11 years old, the first astronauts landed on the moon. This was an amazing achievement for scientists and explorers. Many Americans, including Ellen, watched coverage of the event on television. Ellen watched the moon landing

STELLAR!

The mission that brought the first people to the moon was part of **NASA's** Apollo program. The Apollo program lasted from 1961 to 1972.

Astronauts Neil Armstrong and Buzz Aldrin (*pictured*) were the first people to walk on the moon. They placed a US flag on the moon.

with excitement. But even though she was skilled in science, she did not dream of one day traveling to space herself. At the time, there were no female astronauts. So, Ellen did not imagine it as a possible career path.

Ellen continued to focus on her studies, which included music. She became an excellent flute player. She even gave flute lessons for $10 an hour. Ellen also had a job at her high school, Grossmont High in La Mesa. Ellen stayed after class each day and worked in the school office. She earned $2 an hour for this work.

The difference in pay between Ellen's two jobs taught her an important lesson. Learning how to work in the office was easier than learning to play the flute. But she was able to earn more money with her flute skills than her office skills. This made learning the flute worth the time and effort. Ellen realized that putting time and effort into things is valuable.

Ellen put this realization to work in school. And it paid off. In 1975, Ellen graduated from Grossmont High at the top of her class. She would continue to work hard for what she wanted her entire life.

Ellen (*circled*) played in the Grossmont High School orchestra.

Math, Science, Engineering

After high school, Ochoa was accepted at San Diego State University in California. She wanted to study science or math there. At the time, women were often discouraged from studying these subjects. But Ochoa drew inspiration from her female high school teacher, Paz Jensen. Jensen had taught Ochoa calculus, an advanced branch of math.

Ochoa took calculus in college too. Ochoa also realized most of the other calculus students were taking the courses as a requirement. But she took them for fun!

As Ochoa chose a focus of study in college, she thought about her skill in math. She spoke to a professor who told her calculus was used a lot in **physics**. Ochoa decided to major in this branch of science. In 1980, she graduated from San Diego State University with a **bachelor's degree** in physics.

Ochoa continued her education. In the fall of 1980, she began attending California's Stanford University to study electrical **engineering**. This field includes a lot of math and science. Ochoa earned a **master's degree** in 1981.

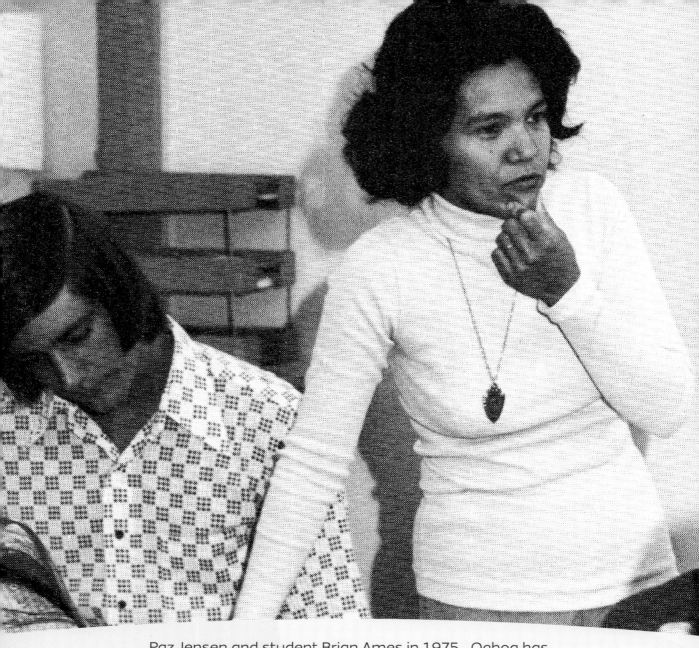

Paz Jensen and student Brian Ames in 1975. Ochoa has said the school didn't offer calculus every year. She felt lucky it was offered when she wanted to take it.

4 Space Inspiration

Ochoa remained in school, studying for a **PhD** in electrical **engineering**. While Ochoa was earning degrees, her mother continued to take one college class at a time. Rosanne graduated from San Diego State University in 1983.

Another woman Ochoa admired also achieved a milestone in 1983. On June 18, 1983, astronaut Sally Ride became the first American woman in space. Ochoa and other women around the nation followed the coverage with awe and excitement. Some of Ochoa's female friends decided to apply to the **NASA** astronaut program. Ochoa wanted to as well. She contacted NASA to find out what the program requirements were.

NASA told Ochoa astronaut candidates must have a degree in science, engineering, or math. So, her **bachelor's** and **master's degrees** fulfilled this requirement. NASA said astronaut candidates must also have three years of related work experience or an advanced degree. Ochoa realized that her PhD would qualify her. Once she completed it, she could apply to become an astronaut. For the first time, Ochoa began to dream of traveling to space.

Ride went on two space missions on the space shuttle *Challenger*.

Astronaut Ambition

In 1985, Ochoa earned her **PhD** in electrical **engineering** from Stanford University. The same year, she began working at Sandia National Laboratories in Livermore, California. There, Ochoa performed research on optics.

Also in 1985, Ochoa applied to **NASA's** astronaut program. The program was competitive and received many applicants. Ochoa was not chosen.

Though she was disappointed about not becoming an astronaut, she had many successes at her job at Sandia. Ochoa and her coworkers applied for patents on three optical inventions. One was granted in 1987. The other two patents were approved in the following years.

Ochoa had found great satisfaction in her career. But she did not give up her dreams of space travel. She continued to work on making herself a better astronaut candidate. This included getting her pilot's license.

In 1987, she applied for NASA's astronaut program again. This time, NASA invited Ochoa to come to Houston, Texas, for an interview at the JSC.

Ochoa in the Sandia optical lab with Don Sweeney (*left*) and George Schils. The three received a patent for their work in 1989.

At the JSC, Ochoa and other astronaut applicants were interviewed and tested for an entire week. Ochoa returned home and waited for **NASA's** decision. Months later, she learned that, again, she had not been selected.

6 NASA

NASA had not selected Ochoa to be an astronaut for the second time. But it had taken notice of her knowledge of optics. NASA offered her a job. In 1988, she became an optical systems researcher at NASA's Ames Research Center in Mountain View, California.

As she had at Sandia, Ochoa achieved great success at NASA. She led a team of 35 other scientists to create optical and computer systems for space missions. Ochoa believes this leadership further helped her chances of becoming an astronaut.

Ochoa has often been asked if she felt her first two applications were failures. But she says she never felt they were. Instead, she thinks they helped her. Ochoa believes NASA pays attention to whether people give up on their dreams. She says not giving up is a great quality for NASA employees and astronauts to have. So is working to improve and trying again.

Since her first application, Ochoa had been improving her skills and gaining experience. This included getting her pilot's license and continuing research into optical systems. She applied to the astronaut program a third time. There were almost

Part of Ochoa's training at NASA included flying in a T-38 jet. The jet provides a similar experience to being in a space shuttle.

2,000 applicants. In 1990, she and 23 others were chosen to become astronauts! She said her feeling when she was chosen was "pure **elation**." She knew becoming an astronaut would change her life.

⑦ Making History

Becoming an astronaut was not the only change for Ochoa. She had met Coe Miles while working at Ames. They got married shortly before Ochoa was accepted to the astronaut program. In July 1990, the couple moved to Houston, Texas, where Ochoa began her astronaut training at the JSC.

The training was very intense. Astronauts must be fully prepared for any situation. Astronaut trainees must learn to solve problems. And if several things go wrong at once, astronauts must know which to address first.

Ochoa and the other astronauts also studied aircraft safety, astronomy, and **meteorology**. They learned about space equipment. They also flew on a special airplane that created reduced gravity. This prepared them to work in **zero gravity**.

In July 1991, Ochoa completed her training. Her graduation was not just a major milestone for Ochoa, but for the entire nation. Ochoa became the first Hispanic female astronaut in history. This historic moment was soon followed by another. Ochoa prepared for her first mission. This flight would make her the first Hispanic female in space.

FEMALE FIRSTS

VALENTINA TERESHKOVA (1937–)
- First woman in space
- Russian astronaut
- Orbited Earth 48 times in three days in spacecraft *Vostok 6*

SALLY RIDE (1951–2012)
- First US woman in space
- Physicist and US astronaut
- Helped shuttle crew members launch satellites and conduct experiments

MAE JEMISON (1956–)
- First African-American woman in space
- Engineer, physician, and US astronaut
- Performed experiments on motion sickness and weightlessness while in space

KALPANA CHAWLA (1962–2003)
- First Indian-American woman in space
- Research scientist, certified flight instructor, and US astronaut
- One of seven crew members who died on space shuttle *Columbia* in 2003

LIU YANG (1978–)
- First Chinese woman in space
- Pilot and Chinese astronaut
- Performed medical experiments in space

8 First Flight

Ochoa's first space flight took place on April 8, 1993. She was one of five astronauts on the space shuttle *Discovery*. It left Kennedy Space Center in Florida at 1:29 a.m. Within ten minutes, the shuttle was orbiting Earth. Ochoa officially became the first Hispanic female in space.

The *Discovery*'s mission was to study the effects of the sun's energy on Earth's climate, environment, and atmosphere. Ochoa was the **mission specialist**. She operated the shuttle's Remote Manipulator System (RMS). The RMS captured an orbiting **satellite** that had been gathering information.

The *Discovery*'s crew also studied the effects of human activity on Earth's atmosphere. At the time, scientists knew human-made chemicals were entering the atmosphere. Some scientists believed these substances were destroying the **ozone layer**. Ochoa and her coworkers determined that chemicals called **chlorofluorocarbons** were in fact destroying the ozone layer. These results

STELLAR!

Ochoa was awarded **NASA's** Space Flight Medal after her 1993 mission. This award is given to every NASA astronaut who travels to space. An astronaut is awarded another medal after each mission.

Ochoa brought her flute on her first space mission.
She played it for the crew and for an educational video.

led to international policy changes. New laws were passed that ended the use of **chlorofluorocarbons**.

Ochoa's space mission made her an inspiration to many. She gave speeches at schools with large Hispanic populations. She also spoke for groups that support women and **minorities** in science careers.

More Missions and Medals

In 1994, Ochoa returned to space on the shuttle *Atlantis*. She was the **payload** commander on this eight-day trip. Ochoa was very focused on her crew's mission. However, she also wanted to take time to enjoy the amazing experience. This included looking at Earth from space. Ochoa says this is a spectacular sight.

Ochoa received her second Space Flight Medal from **NASA** upon her return. In 1995, she also received its Outstanding Leadership Medal. And in 1997, NASA awarded Ochoa its Exceptional Service Medal.

In 1999, Ochoa traveled to space for a third time. This trip was on the *Discovery*. Ochoa was the **mission specialist**. During this mission, Ochoa and her crewmates became the first astronauts to dock their shuttle to the International Space Station (ISS).

The ISS was empty at the time. It was in the process of being prepared for a crew to live aboard it. The *Discovery* astronauts dropped off four tons (3.6 t) of supplies and equipment.

Three years later, Ochoa took her fourth space flight, again acting as mission specialist. Her crew returned to the ISS on

Ochoa looks out a window on the ISS.

the space shuttle *Atlantis*. An international crew now lived on the ISS. The ISS crew worked with the *Atlantis* crew to add new equipment to the ISS.

Growing Responsibilities

As Ochoa's space experience grew, so did her family. She and Miles had two sons. Ochoa's children were very young during her space travels. During her last flight, her older son was three. Her younger son turned two while Ochoa was in orbit.

Ochoa's children associated their mother with space travel. They did not realize that few women worked in space-related fields. According to Ochoa, one of her sons asked her, "Mom, can boys be astronauts or just girls?"

Although Ochoa no longer went on missions, her career at **NASA** was far from over. In December 2002, Ochoa was named Deputy Director of Flight Crew Operations at the JSC. Ochoa continued to work hard. Four years later, she became Director of Flight Crew Operations. In 2012, Ochoa once again made history. She was named Director of the JSC. She was the first director who was Hispanic and the second who was female.

STELLAR!

Ochoa has said she misses **zero gravity** when not in space. She says lack of gravity makes some tasks harder but many others easier. She also says feeling weightless is fun.

Ochoa with her husband and their sons, Wilson (*standing*) and Jordan

11 Ochoa's Legacy

Ochoa accomplished many firsts as a female astronaut and space leader. In 2015, she was awarded the National Space Grant Distinguished Service Award. She has also earned **NASA's** Distinguished Service Medal. This is NASA's highest honor.

In 2017, Ochoa entered the US Astronaut Hall of Fame. She was still Director of the JSC, managing about 13,000 employees. Ochoa retired in May 2018, feeling she had completed a fulfilling 30-year career at NASA. After her retirement, she and her husband moved to Idaho.

Ochoa learned a great deal about space during her career at NASA. But she believes scientists are just now beginning to learn what benefits space may provide. Ochoa also feels that **minorities** and women could be better represented in space exploration. It is as a pioneer in this area that she is best known.

During Ochoa's career, she received thousands of letters from children. Many of them became interested in space careers after learning about her. "If that's the kind of **impact** that NASA can have and I can **personify** that, that's a wonderful **legacy**," she said in 2011.

Ochoa plays with the band at Ellen Ochoa Middle School in Pasco, Washington. The school is one of six US schools named in her honor.

Ochoa encourages students to follow their dreams. She credits learning as the key to success. "Don't be afraid to reach for the stars," she says. "I believe a good education can take you anywhere on Earth and beyond."

Timeline

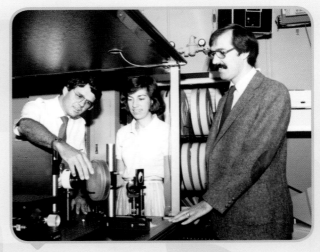

Ellen Ochoa is born on May 10 in Los Angeles, California.

1958

Ochoa completes her PhD in electrical engineering at Stanford University.

1985

1975
Ellen graduates at the top of her class from Grossmont High in La Mesa, California.

1988
NASA hires Ochoa to work at its Ames Research Center.

1991
Ochoa completes astronaut training, becoming the first Hispanic female astronaut in history.

Ochoa travels to space on *Discovery*. She is the first Hispanic woman in space.

1993

Ochoa becomes Director of Flight Crew Operations.

2006

Ochoa becomes a member of the US Astronaut Hall of Fame.

2017

2002

In December, Ochoa is named Deputy Director of Flight Crew Operations at the JSC.

2012

Ochoa is made the Director of the JSC. She is the first Hispanic person and second woman to hold the title.

Glossary

bachelor's degree—a college degree that is usually earned after four years of study.

chlorofluorocarbon—a gas that was once commonly used in many products such as spray cans and cleaning products.

elation—a feeling of great happiness, joy, or pride.

engineering—using scientific methods to design and create new products or systems. Someone who works in engineering is an engineer.

heritage—something handed down from one generation to the next.

impact—a strong effect on something.

legacy—something important or meaningful handed down from previous generations or from the past.

master's degree—a college degree that is usually earned after one or two years of additional study following a bachelor's degree.

meteorology (mee-tee-uh-RAH-luh-jee)—a science that deals with weather and the atmosphere.

minority—a racial, religious, or political group that differs from a larger group in a population.

mission specialist—an astronaut who has advanced scientific, medical, or engineering training. Mission specialists are often in charge of any experiments that are part of their missions.

NASA—National Aeronautics and Space Administration. NASA is a US government agency that manages the nation's space program and conducts flight research.

ozone layer—a gas layer that surrounds Earth and blocks out certain sun rays.

payload—a spacecraft's cargo, such as passengers or equipment needed for experiments.

personify—to have a lot of a particular ability or quality.

PhD—doctor of philosophy. Usually, this is the highest degree a student can earn.

physics—a science that studies matter and energy and how they interact.

satellite—a manufactured object that orbits Earth. It relays scientific information back to Earth.

sibling—a brother or a sister.

zero gravity—the absence of weight, as in outer space.

ONLINE RESOURCES

Booklinks
NONFICTION
NETWORK
FREE! ONLINE NONFICTION RESOURCES

To learn more about Ellen Ochoa, visit **abdobooklinks.com**. These links are routinely monitored and updated to provide the most current information available.

Index